ABOVE THE HOLY LAND

ABOVE THE HOLY LAND

Israel from the Air

Text and Photographs by Baron Wolman

Chronicle Books ▪ San Francisco

Printed in Japan.

Library of Congress Cataloging-in-Publication Data
Wolman, Baron.
    Above the Holy Land.

    1. Israel—Aerial photographs.   2. Israel—
Description and travel—Views.   I. Title.
DS108.5.W65   1987   915.694′054′0222   87-10300
ISBN 0-87701-409-4

Editing: Deborah Stone
Book and cover design: Nielsen/O'Brien, San Francisco
Composition: TBH/Typecast Inc., Cotati, California
Map illustration: Yuri Anne Tateishi

The photographs on pages 42 and 132 are courtesy
of the Matson Collection, The Episcopal Home,
Alhambra, California

Israeli Edition, Steimatzky Ltd., P.O. Box 628, Tel Aviv
61006, Israel. Telephone: (3) 622536

Distributed in Canada by
Raincoast Books
112 East 3rd Avenue
Vancouver, B.C.
V5T 1C8

10 9 8 7 6 5 4 3 2 1

Chronicle Books
One Hallidie Plaza
San Francisco, California 94102

PHOTOGRAPH ON PAGE 2: *Nearly 1500 feet above the
Dead Sea stand the partially restored ruins of Masada,
the fortress where Jewish Zealots held out against
Roman attackers for three years from A.D. 70–73.
Rather than be captured when Masada was eventually
overrun, the 960 Zealots chose to die by their own hands.*

This book is dedicated with affection, love, and gratitude to my mother, whose lifelong commitment to Israel inspired me to take my first flight above the Holy Land, and who, of course, made it all possible in the first place.

Mildred Baron Wolman Burstein, 1912–1987

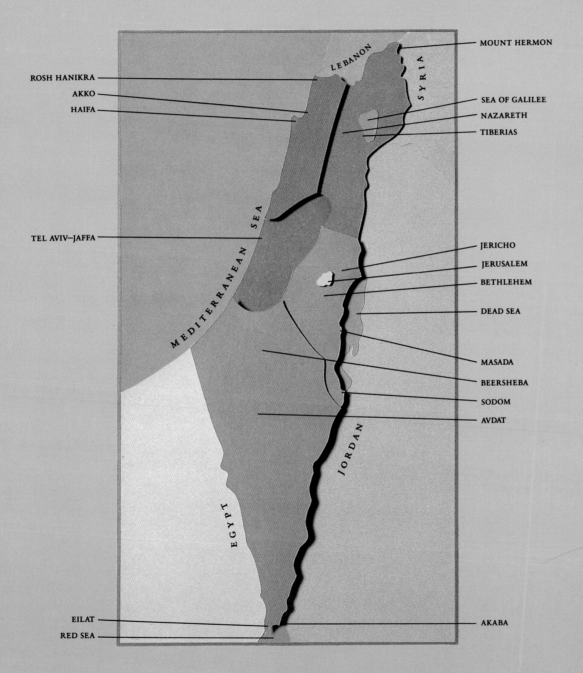

ROSH HANIKRA

AKKO

HAIFA

TEL AVIV–JAFFA

MEDITERRANEAN SEA

LEBANON

SYRIA

MOUNT HERMON

SEA OF GALILEE

NAZARETH

TIBERIAS

JERICHO

JERUSALEM

BETHLEHEM

DEAD SEA

MASADA

BEERSHEBA

SODOM

AVDAT

JORDAN

EGYPT

EILAT

RED SEA

AKABA

JERUSALEM

TEL AVIV–JAFFA, SAMARIA
AND THE CENTRAL COAST

NORTH TO HAIFA AND
BEYOND

ON AND AROUND THE
SEA OF GALILEE

EAST FROM JERUSALEM
TO THE DEAD SEA

ACROSS THE NEGEV TO
EILAT AND THE RED SEA

Contents

Introduction — Israel from the Air   8

Jerusalem, The 5000-Year-Old City   11

Tel Aviv–Jaffa, Samaria and the Central Coast   35

North to Haifa and Beyond   59

On and Around the Sea of Galilee   81

East from Jerusalem to the Dead Sea   103

Across the Negev to Eilat and the Red Sea   125

Israel from the Air

Imagine a passion. Imagine two passions. Imagine them combined into a single career. Because I love to fly and I love to make photographs, you may then understand why there is little I would rather do than take pictures from the sky.

From the moment my high school pal, Harlan Pollock, suggested I shoot Israel from the air, I knew I would do it. It was a natural. There is no lack of interest in the country. Israel—the Holy Land—is always in the news; many people are deeply concerned about its destiny. But I had no real perception of how the land actually looked. In my ignorance I conjured up sand-swept deserts, brave soldiers, hot-shot jet pilots, and political unrest.

One quick trip and one short photo-flight later I realized how much there is to the Holy Land. Not only is it geographically diverse and as such, very photogenic, Israel is also tightly tied to my own notion of existence. From the day I was born, I learned about God and correct behavior; in Sunday school I read the well-known Bible stories. And I developed a personal ethic grounded in that God and in those stories, most of which took place in the Holy Land.

Suddenly, here I was, flying over the very spot that, without my knowing it, had such an effect upon the person I had become, not in a religious sense, per se, but in the way I encounter life and question it—my fears and hopes, my superstitions, and my belief in one God.

The project thus became infused with an additional emotional quo-tient, which led me to this goal: With the unique perspective that aerial photography offers, I would represent Israel, the Holy Land, in all its variety, attempting to bring it to life for others whose spiritual roots also lie there.

Because Israel is in a constant state of military preparedness, photographers are not permitted to pick up their Nikons, climb in the nearest Cessna, and head out cross-country to do a little afternoon shooting from the air. There are rules.

First, the government has to approve the project in general. Then the military has to approve the shooting schedule in particular. Then the Air Force has to approve the specific flight. The photographer must agree not to photograph sensitive sites, no matter how innocuous they may appear. And all film must be processed and then submitted to the military before it leaves the country.

Under the circumstances, the requirements are reasonable enough. Most permissions were granted quickly and with a minimum of red tape. The censor cut only one frame from nearly five thousand exposures.

Aerial photography in the Holy Land was a familiar experience because all my pictures were made from a Cessna-172, an exact duplicate of the Cessna I hangar in California. Our flights launched from Sde Dov Airport, a small field north of Tel Aviv's hotel row, where air operations are mixed comfortably among military, commercial, and general aviation flying.

Once the plane and pilot were scheduled, and photo permissions for the particular flight were obtained, there were no surprises. Some areas were occasionally off-limits to over-flights, but for the most part I was allowed to photograph throughout the country. Even reasonable variations in flight plans were usually permitted.

Because I have my own plane and because there are very few restric-

8

tions on flying in the United States, I am spoiled. If I get up in the morning and the weather is good, I'm off. It's as simple as that. Once I know my partner isn't using the plane, nobody decides if, when, or where I go but me.

Not so in Israel. All air space is under positive control. Civilian flights, in particular photo-flights, must be arranged before you know if the weather is going to cooperate. And that was my biggest problem, since weather has a mind of its own. To make matters more complex, the Cessna I used doubled as the morning commute traffic eye-in-the-sky for a Tel Aviv radio station, which meant that other than on weekends, magic morning light was unavailable to me.

In addition my pilot had a very busy schedule: a full-time job in El Al operations at Ben Gurion Airport, the flying traffic reporter, seeding clouds to assure they dropped water before reaching Jordan, hauling goods and people around the country, flying precise mapping missions, and who knows what else.

Given the situation, I think we did quite well. There wasn't as much snow on Mount Hermon as I might have liked. And, since I did my shooting in spring and autumn, I missed some colorful summer fun on and around the Sea of Galilee. But following a fierce rainstorm in November I had one spectacularly clear day when the air was sparkling and visibility virtually unlimited. I could see clearly all the way west to the Mediterranean and north to Syria from my vantage point above Jerusalem.

There are some tricks you learn after a few flights, but basically aerial photography requires nothing more complex than film, a camera with some lenses, and a high-wing airplane with a window that opens. My own equipment consisted of two motor-driven Nikon F-3s, five lenses from 35mm to 180mm, and a polarizing filter. Because there is no Kodachrome processing in Israel, and because the censor had to see all the pictures, I shot the entire book with 50- and 100-speed Fujichrome, which I had processed in Tel Aviv.

The Holy Land lies at the most concentrated focal point of political and religious power in the world. For fifty centuries this territory has been coveted, lost, captured, recaptured, destroyed, rebuilt again and again, era after era. Certainly, there have been relatively long periods of peace and tranquility when arts and commerce flourished, but from a historical perspective, instability is the constant. Modern Israel is lean and powerful, surrounded by very real enemies—today's experience of a trend that began five thousand years ago and shows no signs of abating.

In any event, that's how it appeared to me as I flew back and forth, up and down, between the borders of Israel. My mission was aerial photography, making a series of pictures for this book, a series that I hope conveys a sense of being suspended between yesterday, today, and tomorrow. For the Holy Land is precisely that: a continuum of experience that spans the years, reflecting history in its people, its holy and historical places, and in the land itself.

Jerusalem, the 5000 Year-Old City

Before you see the city, you notice the hills. Distinctly contoured, the hills of Judea are lined with horizontal layers of white rock, as if a cartographer had transferred his topographical map directly onto the earth. From the air you notice how stones have been rearranged by generations of farmers to catch rainwater or define property lines. Small Arab villages appear with regularity, each punctuated by a minaret, a vertical pointer to heaven.

Approaching Jerusalem from the west, the route of flight crosses the terraced Judean hills. In the distance is the Dead Sea; beyond it, the country of Jordan.

And then, Jerusalem. Suddenly, you are flying over ridgetop apartment complexes, over planned developments cut into hillsides, over broad streets sweeping along curves of the hills, over the four-lane highway from Tel Aviv, which links Israel's two most important urban areas.

Jerusalem is located upon and among the hills of Judea, twenty-five-hundred feet above sea level. The focal point is the Old City; everything is seen in reference to this tiny area, which has been inhabited for nearly fifty centuries. Its perimeter is clearly defined by the two-and-a-half-mile stone wall with its battlements, towers, and seven gates. The magnificent golden Dome of the Rock on the Temple Mount is the Old City's most compelling landmark. A closer look reveals the Western Wall of the Second Temple, the Church of the Holy Sepulchre, the Church of the Redeemer, archaeological diggings, and the distinct features of the four religious quarters.

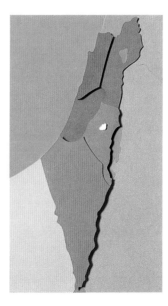

In Jerusalem, a sacred site is more than a house of worship. It is often the very location where events occurred and were subsequently sanctified, events that even in the twentieth century may still determine how we pass our years on this planet.

ABOVE: *There is little random development in the hills of Jerusalem. Large-scale housing projects are carefully planned and often imaginatively designed by noted architects. By law, all buildings must be faced with Jerusalem stone; naturally pastel in color, the stone gives the city a golden glow at daybreak and sunset.*
RIGHT: *Looking west in the early morning from above the Old City of Jerusalem, across Mount Moriah and the golden Dome of the Rock; at lower left are excavations of an archaeological park. Jews and Moslems alike believe the Messiah will someday enter Jerusalem through the sealed Golden Gate.*

14

LEFT: *For 1,900 years, the Western Wall, or Wailing Wall as it is popularly known, has been a sacred place to Jews throughout the world. Around 950 B.C., King David's son Solomon erected a spectacular temple in Jerusalem. In 587 B.C., both Jerusalem and Solomon's temple were destroyed by the Babylonians. In 515 B.C., a second temple was built on the site. Destroyed by the Romans in 63 B.C., it was rebuilt by another Roman, Herod. In 70 A.D., the Temple of Herod was burned to the ground by yet another Roman, Titus, during his siege, capture, and subsequent destruction of Jerusalem. The fifty-foot-high Western Wall is all that remains of the wall that surrounded the temple complex.* RIGHT: *This view of the Old City includes the Jewish Quarter at the lower left, the Moslem Quarter at the upper left, the Western Wall, and the Dome of the Rock.*

LEFT: *A close-up of the Old City's rebuilt Jewish Quarter shows columns to the left marking the entrance to the reconstructed Cardo, a north-south commercial thoroughfare originally built by the Romans. The arch of the Hurva Synagogue faces the Sidna Omar Mosque and the Rambam Synagogue; at bottom center are the four Sephardic synagogues.* RIGHT: *The dominant structure on the Temple Mount is, of course, The Dome of the Rock. Built by caliph Abd el-Malik and completed in 691 A.D., the building stands on the spot where Moslems believe Mohammed made his night ascension to heaven. The holy Moriah rock beneath the gold-plated aluminum dome is thought to be the altar upon which God commanded Abraham to sacrifice his son Isaac.*

Left: *Built on the site of Christ's crucifixion, the twin domes of the venerated Church of the Holy Sepulchre dominate this close-up of the Christian Quarter. To the right is the El Omariya Mosque; to its right the large Church of the Redeemer and the tile-roofed buildings of the Muristan.* Above: *This view of the Moslem Quarter shows the Austrian Hospice in the foreground, the Antonia Fortress at the upper left, as well as the Ecce Homo, Monastery of Flagellation, and Church of Our Lady of the Spasm, each Stations of the Cross along the Via Dolorosa.*

20

LEFT: *This view of the Jaffa Gate, one of seven entrances into the walled Old City, looks down upon the Citadel of Jerusalem. Although it had little to do with King David, the Citadel has come to be known as David's Tower. In fact, it was built by Herod and left standing by Titus when he destroyed the city in 70 A.D. Today the Citadel houses city and folklore museums.* RIGHT: *Built in its present form by Suleiman the Magnificent between 1537 and 1542, the wall surrounding the Old City is forty-feet high and nearly two-and-one-half miles long. The Damascus Gate, seen here, was the southern terminus of the ancient road between Jerusalem and Damascus. Below ground level lie the excavated remains of two earlier city gates.*

RIGHT: *Just east of the Old City, on the Mount of Olives, are the Church of All Nations (bottom left) and the White Russian Church of St. Mary Magdalene (upper right). The Russian Church was built in 1888 by Czar Alexander III in a style popular in Moscow at the time.* FAR RIGHT: *The Intercontinental Hotel sits atop the Mount of Olives, surrounded by the ancient Jewish Cemetery. Below is the main road from Jerusalem to Jericho.*

FAR LEFT: *The Byzantine Dome of the Ascension glows in the late afternoon light; from this spot, Jesus is believed to have ascended to heaven.* LEFT: *The Basilica of the Sacred Heart, built where Jesus "revealed inscrutable mysteries to his disciples," and el-Tur, the Russian Orthodox Ascension Tower.*

Left: *The site of the Virgin Mary's death and Jesus' last Passover meal, Mount Zion is dominated by the Dormition Abbey, dedicated in 1908. It lies adjacent to a building housing the Coenaculum (Latin for* refectory), *venerated as the Hall of the Last Supper. The Coenaculum sits directly above both the Room of the Footwashing as well as what is thought to be the Tomb of King David.* Above: *In the mid-1800s, Czar Alexander II purchased land in Jerusalem to accommodate the numerous pilgrims from Russia. Now known as the Russian Compound, the complex included this cathedral, a hospital, and hostels.*

LEFT: *The world-renowned Israel Museum consists of the Billy Rose Sculpture Garden, the Archaeological Museum, the Bezalel Art Gallery, the Department of Antiquities, and the Shrine of the Book. Shaped like the lid of the earthenware jar in which the Dead Sea Scrolls were found, the dome of the Shrine covers an underground room in which the two-thousand-year-old scroll of the Book of Isaiah is displayed.* RIGHT: *The Israel Museum and Monastery of the Cross are situated at the south end of the Valley of the Cross. The Monastery occupies the site of the tree from which the cross on which Jesus was crucified was made.*

FAR LEFT: *The Knesset,
Israel's House of Parliament,
was dedicated in 1966.
Visitors are welcome to
attend sessions of Parliament or to take guided
tours of the building. Inside
are many works by the
renowned French artist,
Marc Chagall, including
wall and floor mosaics. The
most famous are Chagall's
triple tapestries entitled* The
Creation, Exodus, *and*
Entry in Jerusalem. *In the
foreground is the Wohl
Rose Garden.* LEFT: *The
column at the top of Yad
Vashem — the memorial to
the six million Jews exter-
minated by the Nazis in the
Holocaust — represents the
chimneys of the cremation
ovens.* RIGHT: *Shaped like
the trunk of a fallen tree,
the Kennedy Memorial in
the Peace Forest southwest
of Jerusalem is dedicated to
John F. and Robert F.
Kennedy; it symbolizes lives
cut down so violently.*

29

30

FAR LEFT: *The 800-bed Hadassah Hospital and Medical Center at Ein Karem has a small synagogue, at center, adorned with the famous twelve stained-glass windows by Marc Chagall.* LEFT: *The charming hill village and artist colony of Ein Karem is the birthplace of John the Baptist.* ABOVE: *Near the original Hadassah hospital on Mount Scopus stands a cemetery commemorating British soldiers who died in Palestine during the First World War.*

LEFT: *The Hebrew University on Mount Scopus is one of four campus locations in and around Jerusalem. The university has a combined student body of fifteen thousand and a faculty of more than two thousand teachers.* RIGHT: *In this wide-angle view at dawn from high above the Old City, the Rockefeller Museum is below, the Temple Mount to the left; at upper right are some of the many hotels of West Jerusalem.*

Tel Aviv-Jaffa, Samaria and the Central Coast

Jaffa is a very old city. Traces of civilization from before the Bronze Age have been found there. Biblical accounts of Noah and the Ark, Jonah and the Whale, and St. Peter and Tabitha were set in Jaffa. According to Greek mythology, Perseus rescued Andromeda from the sea monster off Jaffa's coast. And the Cedars of Lebanon for the temple in Jerusalem were brought to the Holy Land through Jaffa's port.

Tel Aviv, by comparison, is an infant, only eighty years old. It was founded in 1909 on the nearby sand dunes as a suburb of Jaffa by a group of Jewish families who wanted to live apart from their work. Tel Aviv grew quickly and in 1923 was officially declared a municipality of its own.

From Ashkelon in the south to the outskirts of Haifa in the north, the spring air is filled with the sweet fragrances of citrus blossoms. In the fertile soil of the Sharon Plain, farm products and citrus grow in abundance. Ironically, much of the area was originally swampland, supporting agriculture only after the marshes were drained by pioneer settlers.

Adjacent to the Sharon Plain in the north is the district of Samaria. In biblical times it was the geographical center of the Holy Land and was then known as the Northern Kingdom. When the city of Samaria—*Shomron* in Hebrew—was founded in 876 B.C., it became the new capital of Israel. During the reign of King Ahab and Queen Jezebel, the Kingdom of Israel achieved great glory. However, the people began to worship Baal and Astarte, turning away from the one God of Israel. In 721 B.C. the city was destroyed by the Assyrians and the kingdom ceased to exist.

Tel Aviv clings to the shore of the Mediterranean, north from the ancient port of Jaffa. Israel's commercial and cultural center, Tel Aviv was created in the early 1900s, and built primarily upon sand dunes. Today its metropolitan population is well over one million.

35

ABOVE: *Tel Aviv's largest seawater swimming pool is adjacent to the largest marina in the Middle East. Kikar Atarim plaza, with its outdoor cafés and souvenir stands, is situated conveniently at the center of hotel row.* RIGHT: *Before there was a Tel Aviv there was Jaffa. Jaffa—the Hebrew word for beautiful—was supposedly founded by Noah's son after the Flood. Predominately Arab, and one of the world's oldest cities, it has been alternately inhabited by Egyptians, Persians, Romans, and Crusaders, to name but a few.*

FAR LEFT: *All beaches in Tel Aviv are public; in good weather—especially on weekends and holidays—they are filled with bathers and sun worshippers. Cafés and restaurants parallel the promenade where strolling and people-watching are popular activities.* LEFT: *The paved and landscaped promenade extends south from the marina nearly to Jaffa. An early-morning jogger passes blue public chairs soon to be filled with tourists and locals reading, looking, or simply passing time by the sea.*

40

LEFT: *A warm weekend afternoon in autumn at Leumi Park in Ramat Gan, a suburb of Tel Aviv. The park features a drive-through safari zoo, as well as extensive recreational facilities for the entire family.* RIGHT: *The Bograhof café and restaurant has an ideal location on the beach between the promenade and the water, directly across from the luxury hotels. On the sidewalk a street-artist performs for an enthusiastic crowd while sunbathers bake in peaceful oblivion.*

41

LEFT: *In the mid-thirties Tel Aviv was more sand than town. This view from that time looks south along the beach from the old stadium at the mouth of the Yarkon River. Camel trains bring sand from beach dunes for processing into cement, the main component of the ever-growing city. Dizengoff Street, soon to become popular with shoppers and the café crowd, is clearly visible in the center of the young city.*
RIGHT: *The same view in 1986. The dunes and camels are gone, the hotels and highrises built, the small town now a metropolis. Only the stadium and the Yarkon River remain. Dizengoff Street is barely discernible, hidden by the many apartment buildings.*

43

LEFT: *In the foreground are the Mann Auditorium, home of the Israel Philharmonic Orchestra, the Habima Theatre with its two stages, and the Helena Rubenstein branch of the Tel Aviv Museum; in the distance, luxury hotels line the Mediterranean.* ABOVE: *The new fountain on Dizengoff Circle was designed by noted Israeli artist Yaacov Agam, who donated it to the city.* RIGHT: *The Dizengoff Center apartment complex and shopping center dominates the intersection of King George and Dizengoff streets. The Agam Fountain can be seen at upper left.*

46

FAR LEFT: *Buses come and go throughout the day and most of the night from Tel Aviv's Central Bus Station. Israel's most common form of public transportation, local and intercity bus service is frequent, efficient, and reasonably priced.*
LEFT: *Weekend soccer games at Bloomfield Stadium in Jaffa draw large crowds. There are several teams and many stadiums throughout the country. Soccer and basketball are the two most popular spectator sports.*

47

48

FAR LEFT: *Savyon, the suburb east of Tel Aviv, is often called the Beverly Hills of Israel. Spacious custom-designed villas with private tennis courts and swimming pools lie adjacent to producing citrus groves.* LEFT: *Northeast of Tel Aviv is the Antipatris Fortress. This area, mentioned in the Old Testament, was populated first by Greeks and then by the Maccabees; Herod the Great finally rebuilt it and renamed it after his father: Antipatris.* ABOVE: *The White Tower of Ramleh was completed in the late thirteenth century; to its right are remnants of Suleiman's eighth century mosque. An Arab community, Ramleh was established toward the end of 700 A.D.*

49

FAR LEFT: *This outdoor market in Ashkelon is one of many common in Israel. Each offers a selection of fresh produce as well as a large variety of household goods like clothing and small utensils.* ABOVE: *Citrus groves on the Sharon Plain east of Ashkelon form a crazy-quilt pattern when seen from above.* LEFT: *Citrus products are harvested in the winter, from mid-December until April. Citrus is an important source of foreign currency, dominating Israel's multimillion dollar agricultural export market.*

51

ABOVE: *The Trappist Monastery of Latrun is located close to the four-lane highway linking Tel Aviv with Jerusalem. The monastery is open to visitors, and the monks sell their famous wine, cheese, and honey.* RIGHT: *From the Mediterranean the land rises toward the east into the hills of Judea. Connected by winding country roads, small villages dot the hilltops. On this clear day the snow-capped peak of Mount Hermon is visible more than a hundred miles to the north.*

54

FAR LEFT: *From this new Israeli settlement village in the hills of Samaria, as with many such communities, residents often must commute to work in the larger coastal cities.* LEFT: *Shomron—also called Samaria—was the capital of the Kingdom of Israel from 880 to 721 B.C. Overrun by the Assyrians, it was subsequently rebuilt by Herod the Great, who renamed it Sebastiya. Under Roman rule the city flourished for two hundred years. This view shows the excavated acropolis in the foreground, with small shops along a columned street at upper right.*

Throughout the Holy Land, minarets mark the Arab communities. In the hills of Judea, Samaria, and the Galilee, from dawn to dusk, five times each day, muezzins call the faithful to prayer from atop these slender towers.

North to Haifa and Beyond

There is a popular saying in Israel: While Tel Aviv plays and Jerusalem prays, Haifa works. Haifa is a factory town, home of the technical university, host to petrochemical and high-tech industries. Its ultramodern port is Israel's most important. Israel's only subway operates in Haifa. The city is also world center of the Bahai religion, a faith based upon unity and brotherhood.

Despite its industries, Haifa is clean and beautiful, situated along the sea and on the perpetually green hills of Mount Carmel. On a clear day in Haifa you can see forever—north across Haifa Bay to Akko, to Nahariya, to Rosh Hanikra, and beyond into Lebanon. The ancient seaport city of Akko was captured by pharaohs and settled by Phoenicians, then occupied by Persians, Greeks, Syrians, and Romans. Akko became the capital of the Crusader kingdom; its sea wall stands today as it did in the twelfth century, and fishermen still sail from the stone piers of the old port.

Most of the shoreline north and south of Haifa is accessible to the public. Broad sunny beaches attract sunbathers and windsurfers. Thanks to the presence of a temple dedicated to Astarte, the Caananite fertility goddess, the seaside town of Nahariya has become known as "honeymoon headquarters." Tidal pools at the Phoenician port of Achziv share the waterfront with a Club Med resort. The chalk-white cliffs of Rosh Hanikra stand sentinel at Israel's northernmost coastal border.

Inland and to the east, Megiddo marks the entrance to the Jezreel Valley, Israel's largest. It is here, the Bible predicts, that mankind's final battle will take place—Armageddon, the ultimate struggle between the forces of good and evil.

From biblical times, the Mediterranean Crusader city of Akko (Acre) was the Holy Land's most important seaport. In the nineteenth century, commercial shipping moved fourteen miles south to Haifa, although substantial fishing activity remains.

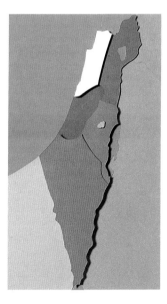

ABOVE: *Akko is popular with tourists who visit its bazaar and museums, beaches and fishing port, and its many archaeological sites. This close-up view into old Akko spans the El Jazzar Wall and the Museum of Heroism to the El Jazzar Mosque.* RIGHT: *Remains of the Roman aqueduct that brought water from Kabri Springs to Akko; the nine-mile structure seen here was rebuilt by the Turk, Pasha el-Jazzar.*

ABOVE: *Once an active Persian port, Achziv is now occupied by Club Med. Adjacent to the popular resort is the public beach and park, with its well-tended Byzantine ruins.* RIGHT: *A single-family home on the beach near Achziv boasts its own private tennis court.* FAR RIGHT: *The city of Haifa is visible from the steep cliffs of Rosh Hanikra on Israel's northern coastal border. A new cable car brings visitors from the restaurant to the sea-level grottoes below.*

62

FAR LEFT: *Founded in 1921, Nahalal is Israel's oldest moshav and birthplace of Moshe Dayan. Each moshav family owns its house and manages its farm; buying and marketing, however, are done cooperatively.*
LEFT: *Strategically sited at the intersection of two vital trading—and military—routes, Megiddo immediately became an important city when it was founded more than four thousand years ago. Archaeologists have unearthed twenty separate cities here, each built on the ruins of its predecessor. The hole at center left is a grain silo from 800 B.C.*

65

LEFT: *Probably Haifa's most photographed landmark, the Bahai Shrine is the World Center of the Bahai faith and the tomb of its founder, Mirsa Ali Mohammed. The Bahai believe that Moses, Christ, Buddha, and Mohammed were messengers from the same God and place considerable emphasis, therefore, upon the brotherhood of man.* RIGHT: *This view is to the west, across Mount Carmel and toward the Mediterranean. At the upper left is the luxury Dan Carmel hotel, below it the Archives of the Bahai religious community, and to the right the golden-domed Bahai Shrine.*

68

FAR LEFT: *An extensive network of fish ponds lies between the Mediterranean and the main Haifa–Tel Aviv highway. Commercially harvested fish represent a major cash crop in Israel. More St. Peter's fish are raised in captivity than are caught in their native habitat, the Sea of Galilee.*
LEFT: *The elegant modern villas of today's Caesarea are powerful contrasts to the two-thousand-year-old Roman aqueduct nearby.*

LEFT: *Named for Augustus Caesar, Caesarea was built twenty centuries ago by Herod the Great. For six hundred years the four-hundred-acre seaport was the local Roman seat of power; Pontius Pilate was in residence here. In the mid-thirteenth century the Crusaders rebuilt the city as a small, forty-acre fortress town. Fifty years later it was destroyed again and subsequently abandoned.* ABOVE: *Both Crusader and Roman ruins have been preserved at Caesarea. Today the restored Roman amphitheater is used for musical and theatrical performances rather than gladiatorial combats.*

LEFT: *The clubhouse of Israel's only golf course, located near Caesarea, faces the putting green and the flag of the 18th hole.*
RIGHT: *The delightful dichotomy of modern Israel is no more evident than in this photo. The tennis courts of today stand in powerful contrast to excavated traces of inhabitants from the distant past.*

73

FAR LEFT: *Just east of the shoreline, between Tel Aviv and Netanya, lies Kibbutz Shefayim. Kibbutzim (plural of* kibbutz*) are no longer wholly agricultural communes; many have turned to manufacturing and other activities for additional income. Shefayim, for example, offers extensive recreation and relaxation facilities for the guests of its 110-room inn.* LEFT: *Adjacent to Shefayim's tiled swimming pools are tennis courts, a soccer field, and two long, brightly colored water slides.*

75

FAR LEFT: *In springtime, near Hadera, new leaves appear on fruit trees. Shadows cast by the afternoon sun enhance the pattern of evenly planted rows.* LEFT: *A crop duster turns across the Alexander River north of Netanya, preparing to spray another citrus grove.* ABOVE: *Luxury villas in Herzliya Pituach hug the bluff overlooking the white sand beaches of the Mediterranean.*

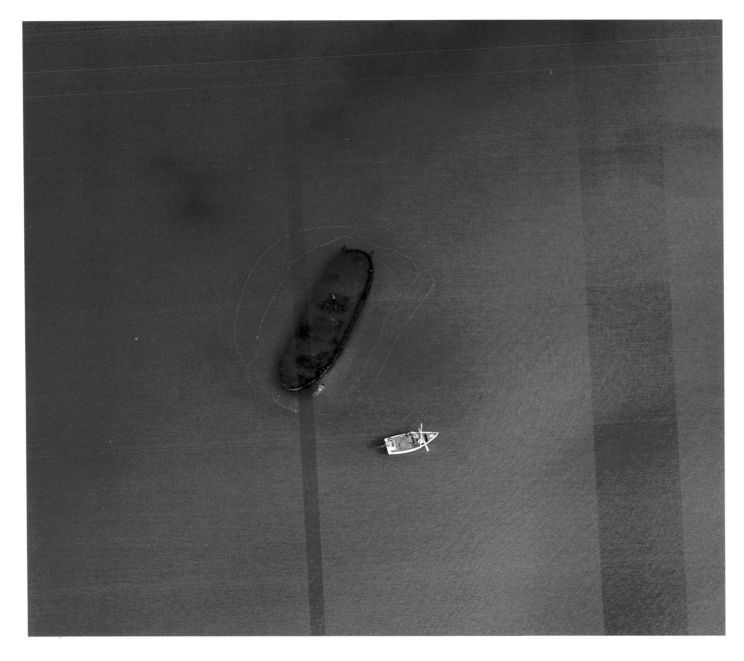

LEFT: *Just offshore at Ga'ash beach lies a sunken boat, a favorite site for snorkeling. Ga'ash is also home of two of Israel's 280 nature reserves.* RIGHT: *Sunny days bring bathers to the seashore in droves. Israel's Mediterranean coastline is more than one hundred miles long and much of it consists of public access beaches.*

On and Around the Sea of Galilee

Israelis call it Lake Kinneret, but to most of the world it is known as the Sea of Galilee. Its territory extends to Israel's northernmost border and includes the Jezreel Valley, the hills of Nazareth and Safed, the Huleh Plain, and the area around the lake. From the Galilee have come ideas and events that have dramatically influenced the course of modern civilization. In Tiberias, Jewish scholars and rabbis codified the Mishna, the book of Jewish traditional law. The mystical teachings of the Cabala were studied and expanded by the wise men of Safed. Christianity, with its beginnings in Nazareth, spread out from the Sea of Galilee, for Jesus lived and taught along its shores.

Israel's very first kibbutz was created on the south shore of the Sea of Galilee. To the north, a century ago, immigrants established the first Jewish settlement in the Galilee since Roman times. Yet Tiberias, the largest city on the lake and now a popular resort, is smaller today than it was during its heyday in the second and third centuries.

Water in the one-hundred-fifty-foot-deep Sea of Galilee is fresh, fed both by underground springs and a series of mountain rivers and streams from the north. The lake is the primary source of fresh water for the entire country—water for drinking and for irrigation. From the Sea of Galilee it is pumped into an elaborate complex of aqueducts and pipelines for distribution throughout the land.

Those who control the Golan Heights in the northeast also control their neighbors. Today, the fertile volcanic soil of the Golan sits untilled, for mines remain in the fields and peace is still tentative.

Founded early in the first century A.D., Tiberias is located on the western shore of the Sea of Galilee. One of Israel's four Jewish holy cities—along with Jerusalem, Hebron, and Safed—Tiberias has become a popular destination for vacationers and pilgrims.

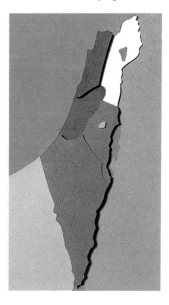

LEFT: *The Sea of Galilee itself is 13 miles long, 7 miles wide, and lies 686 feet below sea level. Here a powerboat speeds past a slow-moving scull in front of remains of a Crusader wall.* ABOVE: *At the southern edge of Tiberias seventeen natural springs pour hot—140°F—mineral water from the depths of the earth. Known for its legendary therapeutic properties, the water has long attracted health enthusiasts. From King Solomon to Herod and the Romans, until today, people have flocked to the spas for soothing baths and treatments.* RIGHT: *Here at Kibbutz Ginossar a perfectly preserved two-thousand-year-old boat was recently discovered, one that could well have been used at the time Christ lived on these shores of the Galilee. Ginossar's guest house also offers travelers 170 rooms of luxury accommodations.*

82

LEFT: *Tour boats from Tiberias dock in front of the Franciscan monastery at Capernaum. When Jesus left Nazareth, he came to Capernaum, where he called his first disciples and preached in the adjacent synagogue. He is said to have worked many of the miracles recounted in the New Testament here.*

RIGHT: *In this close-up of the synagogue at Capernaum, small enclosures can be seen around the main structure; these are thought to be the humble dwellings of local fishermen. The current synagogue is believed to have been constructed around 400 A.D. on the exact site of the synagogue where Jesus was supposed to have taught. At lower right is a partial view of the Octagon of St. Peter, with rooms where Jesus may have actually stayed.*

RIGHT: *Rising above the Sea of Galilee is the Mount of Beatitudes, on whose slopes Jesus delivered his Sermon on the Mount, proclaiming, "Blessed are the meek, for they shall inherit the earth."* FAR RIGHT: *The Franciscan Church of the Beatitudes commemorates the Sermon on the Mount. Its octagonal shape symbolizes the first eight beatitudes, while its dome represents the ninth, in which Jesus spoke to those who were persecuted for believing in his teachings. The structure behind the church is a pilgrim hostel.* OPPOSITE PAGE: *Here the Jordan River and its tributaries flow into the Sea of Galilee. A mixture of farmland and swamps, this is also the site of the Jordan River Park and the Beit Saida Nature Preserve.*

LEFT: *The Kinneret Sailing Company operates ferry service across the Sea of Galilee — known as Lake Kinneret in Israel — from Tiberias to Kibbutz Ein Gev. The annual spring Music and Folklore Festival held in Ein Gev is so popular that the kibbutz had to build a three-thousand-seat concert hall to house the performances.* RIGHT: *Established in 1909 by Russian emigrés, Kibbutz Degania was the first of Israel's more than two-hundred-fifty kibbutzim. It was here, too, that the ideological basis for kibbutz life was first articulated: a village of no private wealth, a communal settlement responsible for all needs of members and their families.*

LEFT: *In this view across the lush lower Jordan River Valley, south of the Sea of Galilee, the Jordanian hills can be seen in the distance. From those hills flows the Yarmuk River, whose waters join the Jordan's for the sixty-mile journey through the Jordan Valley to the Dead Sea.* ABOVE: *A date palm grove flourishes on an agricultural kibbutz in the Jordan Valley.*

92

FAR LEFT: *High on a hill, one thousand feet above the Jordan River Valley, the Crusader castle Belvoir stands guard. Built in 1140, the thirty-two-acre fortress is surrounded on three sides by a moat thirty feet deep and sixty feet wide.* LEFT: *The great Roman amphitheater at Beit Shean once seated more than five thousand spectators. According to archaeologists Beit Shean was first settled thirty-five hundred years before Christ. Philistines, Egyptians, Jews, Romans, and Arabs all inhabited the area during its more than five-thousand-year history, one rich with stories of extended prosperity.*

LEFT: *Jesus spent most of his early life here in Nazareth. Situated in the lovely hills of the lower Galilee, Nazareth is a town of more than twenty churches; it is a religious community populated by Christians and Arabs. The most prominent of the churches is the massive Church of the Annunciation, at center.* RIGHT: *The Church of the Annunciation was completed in 1965. It is actually the fifth church to be built on the site, in the spot where an angel appeared to the Virgin Mary with the message that God had chosen her to bear His son.* FAR RIGHT: *Not far from Nazareth is the Arab village of Kfar Kana. Here, Jesus is said to have worked his first miracle, turning water into wine at the wedding of a poor family. The Franciscan church at upper left supposedly marks the location of that ceremony.*

95

FAR LEFT: *The transfiguration of Christ is thought to have occurred atop Mount Tabor, two thousand feet above the Jezreel Valley. Here the disciples Peter, James, and John first experienced Jesus in godlike form, bathed in white light. The Basilica of the Transfiguration is the large church in the center.* LEFT: *Fresh water travels in the aqueducts of the National Water Carrier from the Sea of Galilee to the headwaters of the Yarkon River near Tel Aviv. From there it is piped east to Jerusalem and south to the desert, where it brings life to the otherwise arid land.*

RIGHT: *The land must be cleared of stone before crops can be grown. Long narrow sheets of plastic cover young plants, retaining moisture and discouraging hungry birds.* FAR RIGHT: *The ruins of Nimrod Castle sit high in the foothills of Mount Hermon. Nimrod was one of a line of several fortresses extending down the mountain to the coast. Its first inhabitants were the Assassins, also known as the Hashashim, a Moslem sect fond of hashish.* OPPOSITE PAGE: *In the foreground is the Huleh Nature Reserve, the last 600 acres of what was formerly a 12,000-acre, malaria-infested swamp. Drained in the mid-1950s, the Huleh Valley has become a fertile, highly productive agricultural area.*

99

ABOVE: *Safed, nearly three thousand feet above sea level, is a holy city, artist colony, source of the mystical teachings of the Cabala, and cool summer resort town.*
RIGHT: *Also three thousand feet above sea level, the freshwater pool of Birket Ram is located only five kilometers from Syria. To the right are the slopes of the Golan Heights and in the background to the left is 9,200-foot-high Mount Hermon, Israel's northeasternmost border. Often snow-capped in the winter, Mount Hermon is a popular ski area.*

East from Jerusalem to the Dead Sea

These days the Jericho road is well-paved and fast. On an ancient trail that once separated the biblical tribes of Judah and Benjamin, traffic speeds by the Inn of the Good Samaritan and past Bedouin tents on the descent from Jerusalem into the Jordan Valley. At Mile 18 the highway drops below sea level. To the north is the oasis city of Jericho, which, according to archaelogists, has been settled continuously from about 8000 B.C., the Middle Stone Age. To the south, fed with fresh water from the Jordan River, is the Dead Sea, thirteen-hundred feet below sea level and the lowest point on the surface of the earth.

Dusk falls in the Judean Wilderness. An international border bisects the Dead Sea from north to south; in the foreground is Israel, in the background the Kingdom of Jordan.

In Hebrew, the Dead Sea is known as *Yam Hamelach*, the sea of salt, for its waters carry ten times the salt of the Mediterranean. Nothing lives in the waters of the Dead Sea and bathers cannot sink in it. Yet its high iodine and sulphur content are ideal in the treatment of skin diseases and its abundant minerals are invaluable as fertilizer.

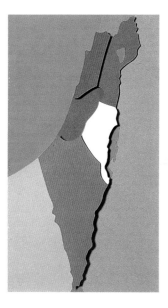

Between the hills of Judea and the Dead Sea is the wilderness of the Judean desert. At once beautiful and forbidding, the area has long given shelter and refuge to religious and political leaders, hermits, and rebels. Here Jesus meditated, David hid from King Saul, and Bar Kochba led a Jewish uprising against the Romans. After nearly two thousand years, the desert yielded a prize, the Dead Sea scrolls. Perfectly preserved at Qumran in earthenware jars, these were the writings of the Essenes, a sect of ascetic Jews that in 150 B.C. split from mainstream Judaism. From their readings of the scrolls, scholars now believe that Essene Jewish philosophy had considerable influence upon the origins of Christianity.

ABOVE: *The Greek Orthodox monastery of Karantel northwest of Jericho perches halfway up the Mount of Temptations. Jesus is said to have fasted here for forty days after being baptized by John the Baptist.* RIGHT: *Atop the Mount of Temptations, a steep climb up from Karantel, are the ruins of Chariton's chapel.* FAR RIGHT: *Just off the main road between Jerusalem and Jericho is the Moslem mosque of Nabi Musa. The mosque was built in 1269 over what Moslems believe is the tomb of Moses. Nearby are the mounds of graves of Moslems who chose to be near Moses in death.*

FAR LEFT: *Mar Saba is eleven miles east of Bethlehem. This Greek Orthodox monastery, open only to men, was founded in 492 A.D. by Saba, a religious hermit who chose the solitude of the desert as his shrine.*

LEFT: *Deep in the gorge of Wadi Kelt is the Greek Orthodox monastery of St. George. Founded in the fifth century, it is built on three levels: churches on the two upper tiers and monks' tombs and storerooms on the lower.*

FAR LEFT: *Scholars believe that Jericho has been inhabited for nearly ten thousand years. In 1860 archaeologists began digging in the area at far right, eventually uncovering twenty layers of successive settlements dating from the Middle Stone Age. An oasis situated 825 feet below sea level, Jericho is blessed with a good supply of fresh spring water, a mild climate, and fertile soil. This fortunate combination produces an abundance of subtropical fruits such as dates, bananas, papayas, and even citrus.* ABOVE: *In 37 B.C. Herod the Great built himself a palace and tomb inside the top of Frank Mountain. Although Herod is said to have died in Jericho thirty-three years later and to be buried here at Herodion, archaeologists have never found his grave.* LEFT: *The round form at upper left is one of the four watchtowers guarding Herodion. Also within the walls stood a synagogue, apartments, hot baths, and a magnificent open courtyard.*

FAR LEFT: *Bethlehem is famous as the birthplace of both King David and Jesus. The red-tile-roofed church at upper right is the Church of the Nativity; the open space in front of it is Manger Square. Across the Square is the Omar Mosque; also visible are Syrian and Evangelical churches, as well as Greek Catholic and Salesian monasteries.* LEFT: *The holy city of Hebron has been occupied since the time of the Canaanites. The Jewish Patriarchs — Abraham, Isaac, and Jacob — are buried here in the Cave of Machpelah. Since Abraham is an accepted ancestor of both the Jews and Moslems, the Mosque of Abraham was built directly above Machpelah. Sarah, Rebecca, and Leah, the wives of the Patriarchs, are also buried in the cave.*

III

ABOVE: *The road from Jerusalem to Hebron winds through the terraced Berakha Valley. Stones cleared from the land are placed in piles, dividing the land into small plots. These stone fences also control erosion and help save water from the area's sparse rainfall.* RIGHT: *East of Hebron, the Hills of Judea descend to the Dead Sea and Jordan. The Judean Wilderness is also visible beyond the terraced hills in this view toward Masada.*

112

LEFT: *Saltwater from the Dead Sea is piped to these large ponds on its north shore. Heated by the sun nearly to boiling point, the hot brine drives turbines which turn generators to produce electricity.* RIGHT: *The midday sun paints Kibbutz Ein Gedi in monochromatic hues. Situated midway along the western shore of the Dead Sea, this biblical oasis is also a national park, the Ein Gedi Reserve, whose canyons are filled with wildlife and pools of cool water. In addition to agricultural activities, the Ein Gedi Kibbutz operates a guest house featuring saltwater spas and thermal treatments from nearby sulphur springs.*

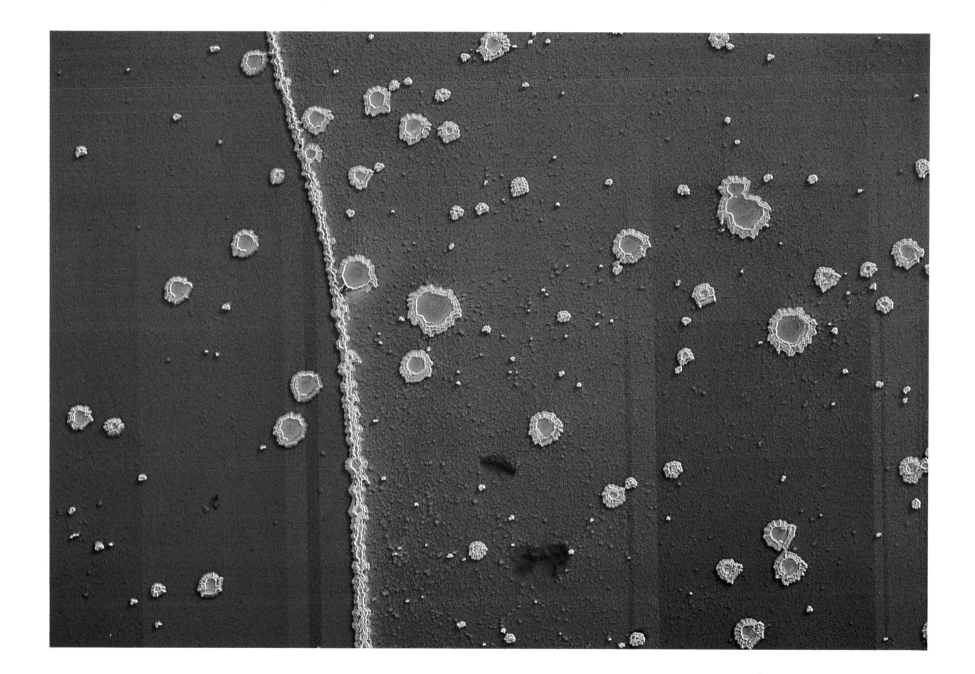

116

LEFT: *Seen from above, salt formations in the shallow waters of the Dead Sea resemble a petri dish of microscopic organisms, or the canvas of a minimalist painter.* ABOVE: *The mineral waters of the hot springs at Ein Bokek have long been renowned. Cleopatra sent her slaves to gather its mud and waters for her beauty treatments; today hotels, clinics, and spas cater to the many visitors drawn to the healing mineral, salt, sulphur, and mud baths. Bathers come to the beaches of Ein Bokek to float in the Dead Sea amid the salt formations.*

LEFT: *Chlorine, bromine, sulphate, sodium, potassium, calcium, and magnesium are harvested in wide blue-green farms at the southern end of the Dead Sea. Contained by dikes, water evaporates in the hot sun so that chemicals can be more easily gathered, processed, and shipped.*
RIGHT: *This view of the Judean desert is near Sodom, the sinful biblical city upon which "the Lord rained fire and brimstone," and where Lot's wife was turned into a pillar of salt. The dry creek bed winds eastward toward the Dead Sea.*

LEFT AND RIGHT: *In 42 B.C., when Jerusalem fell, Herod the Great fled with his family to Masada in the Judean wilderness. By 31 B.C., he had built a walled fortress upon this twenty-acre mountaintop, nearly 1500 feet above the Dead Sea. Masada was also Herod's palace, complete with gardens, royal apartments, swimming pool, bathhouse, administrative offices, barracks, and vast storehouses. The close-up shows the north palace in detail. From left to right are its three terraces, living quarters, baths, storehouses, administrative buildings, synagogue (added later by the Jewish Zealots), and quarry.*

LEFT AND FAR LEFT: *After Herod's death, Masada eventually became a Roman outpost. By the time the Romans conquered and destroyed Jerusalem in 70 A.D., a group of Jewish patriots had fled to the desert, seized Masada, and settled in. It was here they made their famous stand. For eight months nearly a thousand of these Zealots were under siege. Eventually the 15,000-strong Roman Tenth Legion was able to build a stone and earthen ramp up the western slope to the fortress wall. With the end in sight, 960 defenders chose to die by their own hands rather than be captured. Framed in the foreground by the hills of the Judean desert, Masada is bathed in the last rays of sunlight, casting its massive shadow upon the plain below.*

123

Across the Negev to Eilat and the Red Sea

To many, the desert and the Holy Land are synonymous. Understandably, for the Negev—Israel's southern desert—represents nearly 60 percent of the country's land. At midday, from the air, it is a pastel expanse, seemingly lifeless and hostile. In fact, Israel's desert is alive with activity. Bedouin shepherds roam its hills; irrigated fields are green with vegetables; tourists wander its many historical sites; scientific research projects are conducted in Beersheba and Dimona; and since the Sinai was returned to Egypt, the military has had an extensive presence throughout the area.

Most of the Negev's annual twelve inches of rain fall in the north. In the winter flash floods turn otherwise dry riverbeds into foaming white torrents as water rushes from the desert mountains to the Arava rift and into the Dead Sea.

It is thought that the Negev went dry more than ten thousand years ago. Yet it has long supported civilization. After the Canaanites and the Amalekites came the Nabateans, an ingenious people who skillfully irrigated and cultivated the arid land for nearly five hundred years. Dry again for another thousand years, the Negev became fertile once more under the leadership of David Ben Gurion, Israel's first prime minister.

The Negev is a desert of contrasts and patterns, natural and man-made. From above the contrasts are strong and decisive—green plants against beige sand, plateau against canyon, straight roads against meandering dry creeks. The view is a metaphor for the human spirit's ever-present contrast of opportunity: to make the desert grow, to turn the impossible into reality.

Many Bedouin continue to roam the upper desert. Slowly, however, these wandering herdsmen are becoming less nomadic, replacing camels with automobiles, and adding small permanent structures to their tents.

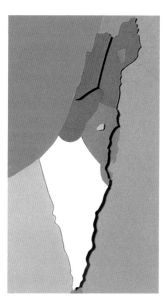

125

FAR LEFT: *At the north end of the Red Sea are the twin cities of Eilat, Israel (foreground) and Akaba, Jordan (background). While Akaba, Jordan's only seaport, is a strategic commercial city, Eilat has become one of Israel's most popular resorts. Israeli and European tourists alike arrive in droves for rest and relaxation at the "Riviera of the Middle East."* LEFT: *Eilat lies at the southern tip of Israel. In biblical times Moses and the Israelites passed through the area. King Solomon's men worked the ancient copper mines nearby, and spice caravans from Arabia rested here. Today modern resort hotels face the beach of the Red Sea and line the shores of the new lagoon. At upper left is Eilat's international airport, with frequent nonstop jet service to and from Tel Aviv and several European cities.*

127

LEFT: *The Red Sea is a paradise for water sports enthusiasts. Boats for charter and rental are available at the marina, as are windsurfing and scuba gear. The floating restaurant shares its structure with a colorful water slide.* RIGHT: *An intimate view of Eilat's King Solomon Hotel. Note the private balconies of the top-floor luxury suites, as well as the ever-present solar collectors, Israel's primary source of hot water. Overnight facilities in Eilat range from five-star resort hotels to inexpensive bungalows.*

FAR LEFT: *A magnificent coral reef south of Eilat has been designated as an official nature reserve. Visitors rent snorkels, masks, and flippers and follow well-marked routes around the reef. For non-swimmers, the Coral World Underwater Observatory seen here provides a dry look at the reef. Sixteen feet below the surface of the Red Sea, windows overlook the reef and the schools of fish inhabiting it. An aquarium and a nautical museum are in the foreground.* LEFT: *The week-long holiday of Passover is a particularly happy one in Israel. Work schedules are abbreviated; many people use the occasion to get away for a few days, usually north to the Sea of Galilee or south to the Red Sea. Along one of Eilat's five beaches, Passover campers gather to relax and play by the water.*

131

ABOVE AND RIGHT: *The oasis of Taba lies five miles south of Eilat. In the mid-1930s there was little visible sign of activity at Taba. Today the Sonesta resort hotel, Eilat's only five-star facility, dominates the area. Beyond the hotel and the beach are Egypt and the mountains of the Sinai. The highway continues south — to the left in the color photo — for nearly one hundred fifty miles to the Sharm-el-Sheikh at the southern tip of the Sinai Peninsula.*

134

FAR LEFT: *This wide view spans northwest across copper mines into the Timna Valley. During King Solomon's time both copper and iron were mined and produced here; some of it was exported from Eilat, fifteen miles to the south. Israel is now developing the area as a national park.*
LEFT: *Copper has been mined at Timna for thousands of years. After King Solomon, both Egyptians and Romans took copper from the land. Substantial reserves still remained; copper and manganese were mined and processed here by Israel until the mid-1970s when falling prices ended current production.*

135

FAR LEFT: *Early attempts to raise cattle in the northern Negev proved unsuccessful. However, thanks to fresh water from the north, it is now possible to grow enough farm produce here to meet domestic requirements and to export in quantity to Europe. Villages, like this one near Ir Ovot, often offer jeep and camel tours into beautiful, hard-to-get-to corners of the desert.* ABOVE: *On the Arava Plain in the southern Negev desert, water has transformed dry sands into productive land. Numerous agricultural villages and kibbutzim grow fruits, vegetables, and flowers on these green, carefully cultivated fields.* LEFT: *A new village is born in the desert near Timna. A perimeter is carved into the sand and buildings erected within. Nearby, farming begins, using advanced agricultural techniques developed by Israeli scientists at the Arid Zone Research Institute.*

137

OPPOSITE PAGE: *One of the newest towns in the Negev, Arad was founded in the early 1960s. Located at an elevation of 2,000 feet above sea level and 3,300 feet above the Dead Sea (visible in the background), the air is cool and pure. The healthy climate attracts tourists to Arad's resort hotels.* FAR LEFT: *The late prime minister of Israel, David Ben-Gurion, is buried on the grounds of Ben-Gurion College near Sde Boker. The college also houses Ben-Gurion's archives and is home to the Arid Zone Research Institute.* LEFT: *Thirty miles south of Beersheba is the kibbutz of Sde Boker. Sde Boker was founded in 1952 by a group of Israelis that included David Ben-Gurion. Tourists are welcome to visit the simple, red-roofed home where he lived until his death.*

RIGHT AND FAR RIGHT:
Two views of the Nabatean-Byzantine hilltop city, Avdat, forty miles south of Beersheba. Established around 300 B.C., and just one of nearly two thousand Nabatean cities, Avdat lay directly on the trade route linking Arabia and the Mediterranean. Caravans laden with perfumes and spices, silks and jewels, were obliged to pass through the area. The Nabateans grew powerful controlling these highways of commerce. OPPOSITE PAGE: *A view into the massive crater of Machtesh Ramon, 7 miles wide and 21 miles long. Beautiful clay rocks over 220 million years old are found at the bottom of the crater.*

RIGHT: *In the Zin desert north of the Avdat ruins is Ein Avdat National Park. Its freshwater pools, cool even in the heat of summer, are filled with water plants and surrounded by reeds and rushes. Wildlife and vegetation abound within the sheer white rock walls of its 400-foot-deep canyon.*
FAR RIGHT: *The chocolate-marshmallow tones of the Tzehiha Hills in the Paran Wilderness reflect the spectacular natural beauty of the desert. The Israelites stopped here in the Paran River Valley en route with Moses from Egypt to the Promised land.*